LISTEN TO YOUR

GW00672306

WHEN YOU HEAR IT STOP, SEEK MEDICAL ATTENTION

The best things in life

ARE ACTUALLY REALLY EXPENSIVE

IF YOU DON'T BELIEVE IN

yourself

YOU'LL NEVER BE LET DOWN

Never.
Give up.

Be Yourself

- NOBODY ELSE WANTS TO BE YOU -

IF AT FIRST YOU DON'T

Succeed

THEN SKYDIVING ISN'T FOR YOU

IT

WILL

PROBABLY

GET

WORSE

LIFE IS THE

journey

NOT THE

destination

and you're lost

IT'S OKAY TO FAIL

AS LONG AS YOU DON'T TRY AGAIN

HAVE A GREAT DAY.

OR DON'T.

nobody ♡ *cares*

MONDAY

HATES YOU TOO!

If life gives you melons,

you might be dyslexic

ALWAYS *believe*
THAT SOMETHING
wonderful

WILL PROBABLY NEVER HAPPEN

EVERY NEW DAY IS
ANOTHER CHANCE AT
failure

Every corpse on Mount Everest was once an extremely motivated person

BELIEVE IN YOURSELF

AND YOU WILL BE

disappointed

IF YOU CAN

Dream it

WHY BOTHER GETTING OUT OF BED?

Everyone has a purpose in life,

YOURS IS TO BE A WARNING TO OTHERS

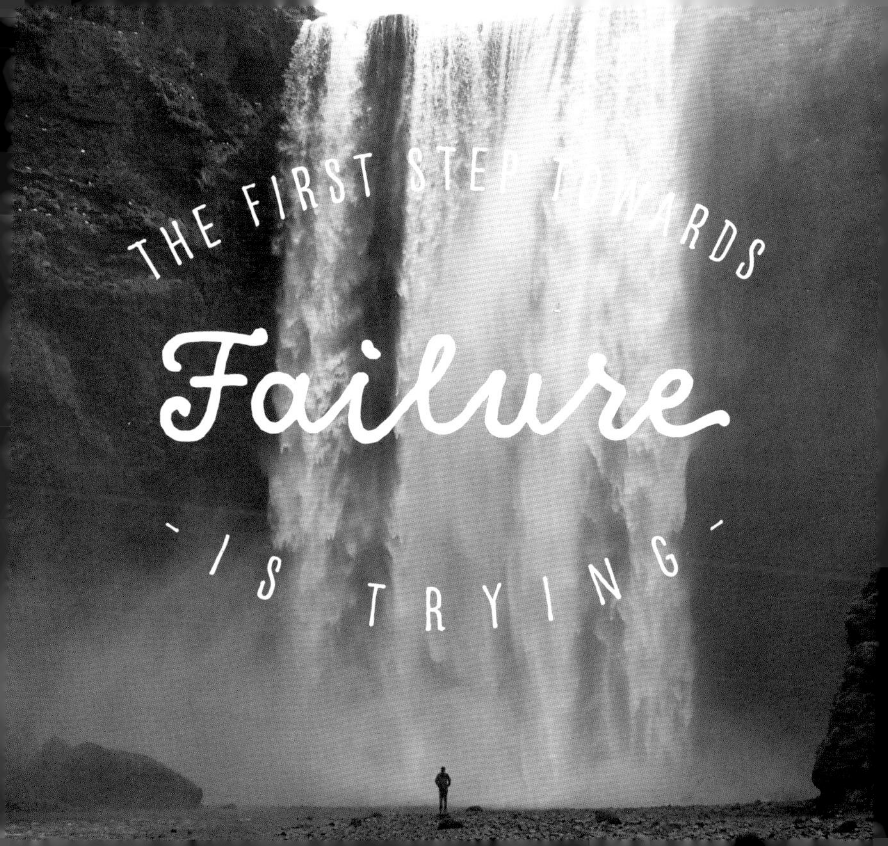
THE FIRST STEP TOWARDS
Failure
IS TRYING

YOU ONLY GET **ONE LIFE**

and you've already ruined it

There are no stupid questions

ONLY STUPID PEOPLE

You're the
reason
somebody is smiling

(BECAUSE YOU'RE A JOKE)

GET LOST IN

nature

AND YOU WILL POSSIBLY DIE

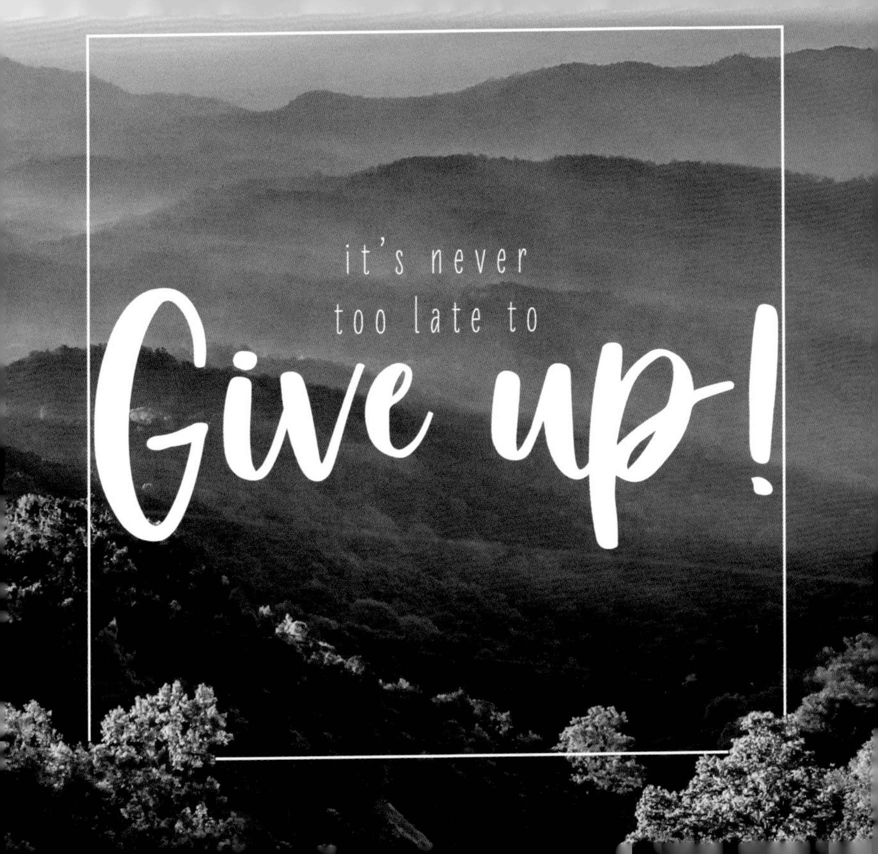
it's never
too late to
Give up!

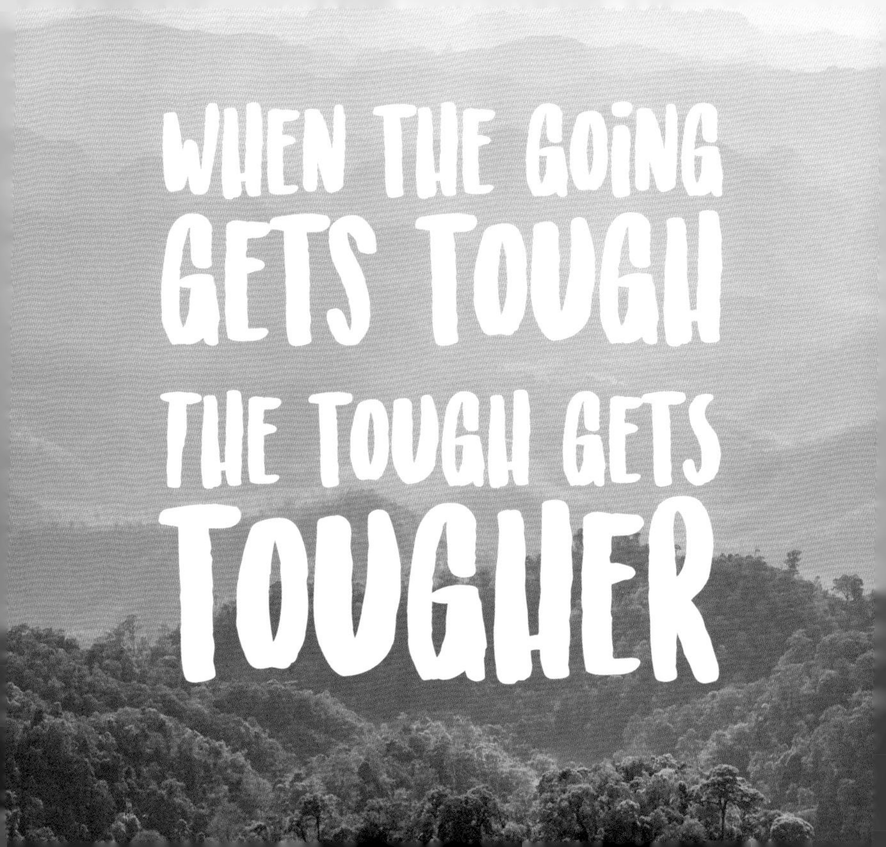
WHEN THE GOING
GETS TOUGH
THE TOUGH GETS
TOUGHER

DO OR DO NOT
nobody cares

IF YOU HATE YOURSELF, REMEMBER THAT YOU ARE

Not Alone

A LOT OF OTHER PEOPLE HATE YOU TOO

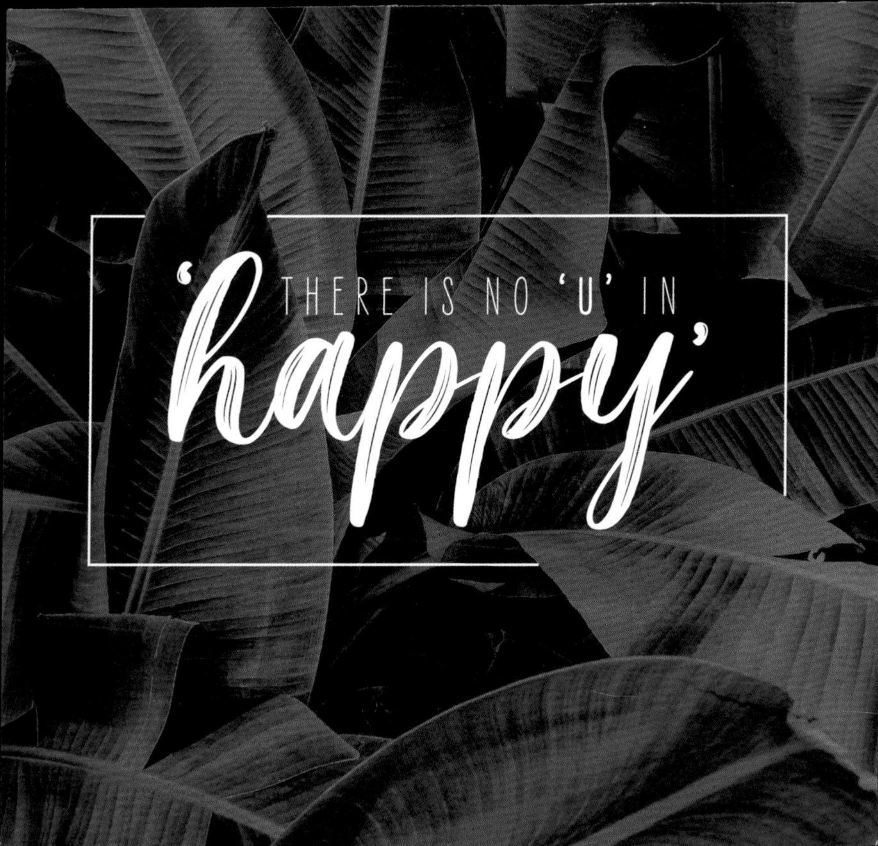
'THERE IS NO 'U' IN
happy'

HOPE IS THE
FIRST STEP TO
DISAPPOINTMENT

free
yourself
of all
prejudice

HATE EVERYONE EQUALLY

WHEN LIFE KNOCKS YOU DOWN

Stay there

IT'S FOR THE BEST

THE WORST THINGS IN LIFE
MAKE YOU WHO YOU ARE

they just haven't happened yet

Will it be easy?

NOPE

Worth it?

ABSOLUTELY NOT

STARTED FROM THE BOTTOM AND NOW LOOK!

- YOU'RE STILL THERE -

IF YOU CAN'T
HANDLE ME
AT MY WORST,

UNFORTUNATELY
THAT'S ALSO
MY BEST

teamwork

ENSURING THAT YOUR HARD WORK
CAN BE RUINED BY SOMEONE ELSE'S
INCOMPETENCE

It's never too late

TO GO BACK TO BED.

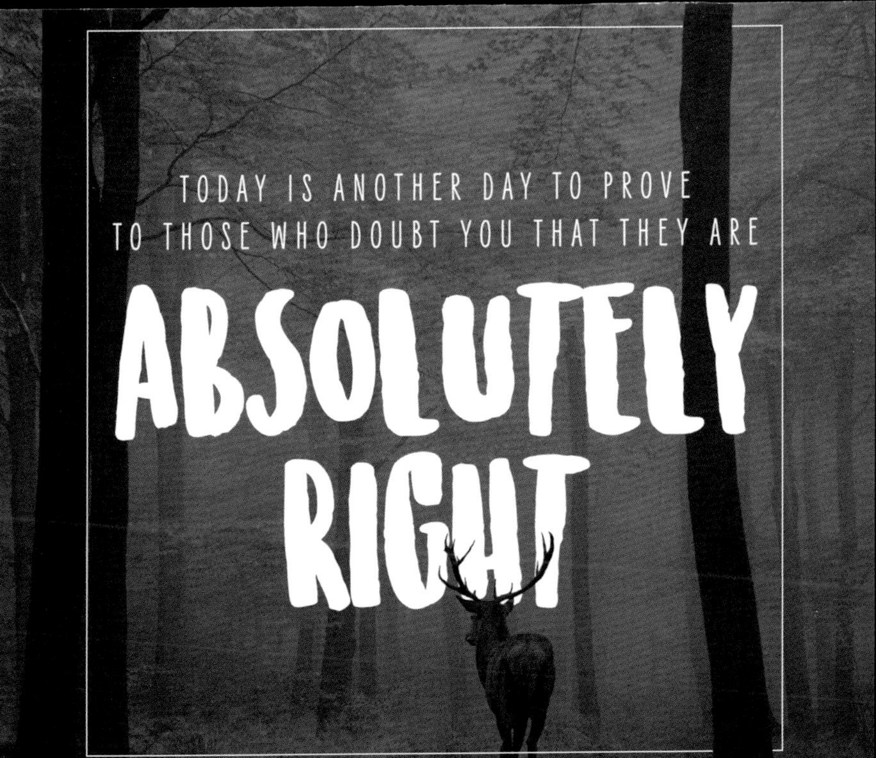
TODAY IS ANOTHER DAY TO PROVE
TO THOSE WHO DOUBT YOU THAT THEY ARE
ABSOLUTELY
RIGHT

Nobody is perfect

SHOOT FOR ADEQUATE

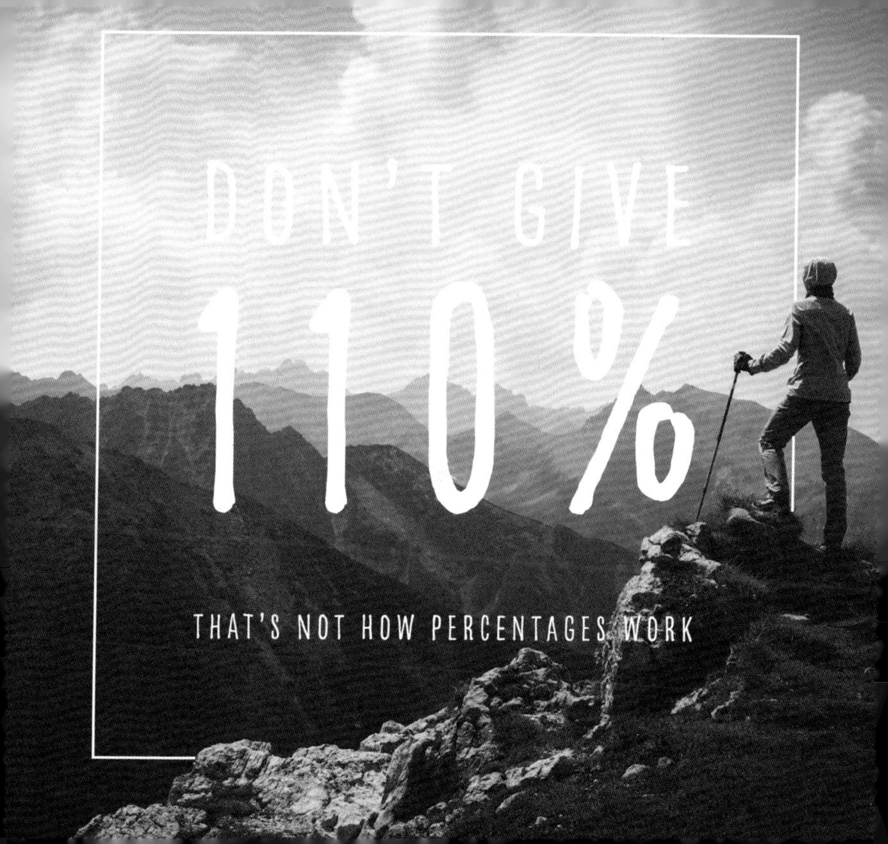
DON'T GIVE
110%
THAT'S NOT HOW PERCENTAGES WORK

THERE IS SOMEONE FOR EVERYONE,

Except You

TODAY IS THE FIRST DAY OF THE REST OF YOUR LIFE

BUT SO WAS

yesterday

AND LOOK HOW THAT TURNED OUT

Start every day with a *goal*
so you always have something to *mess up*

YOUR LIFE CAN'T
FALL APART
IF IT WAS NEVER TOGETHER
TO BEGIN WITH

EVERY TATTOO IS *temporary* BECAUSE WE'RE ALL *slowly dying*

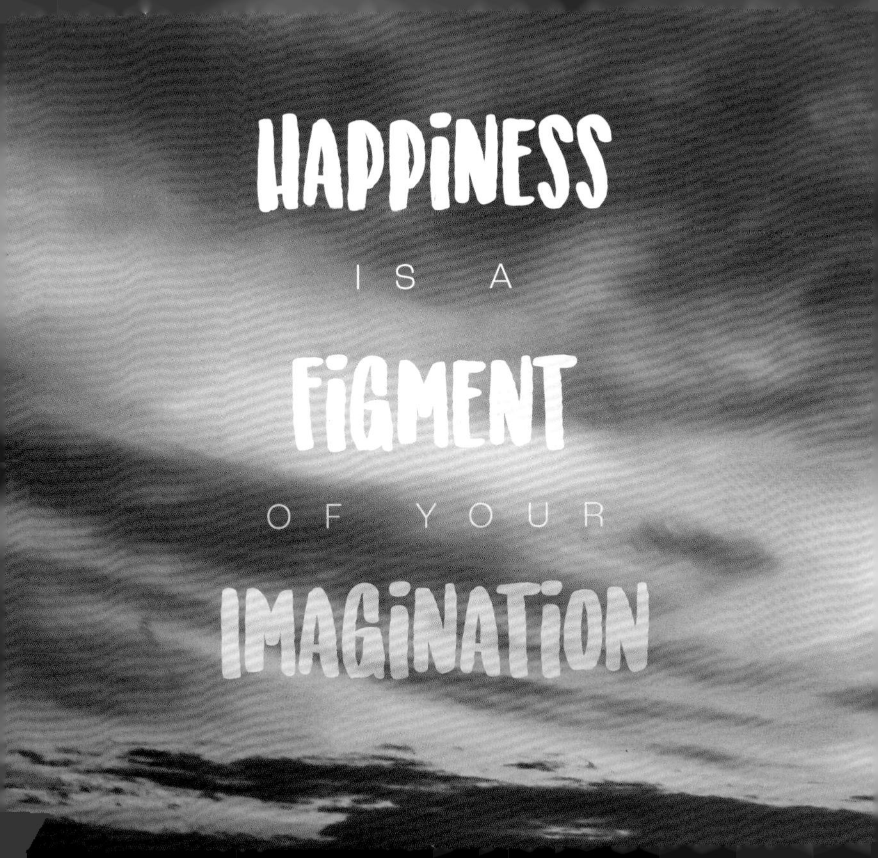
HAPPINESS
IS A
FIGMENT
OF YOUR
IMAGINATION

A JOURNEY BEGINS WITH A
single step
•BUT SO DOES FALLING OFF A CLIFF•